YOU'VE GOT ISSUES

How to gain insight into issues and
take charge of your life

by

Glenn Thomas LCSW

First Edition, Copyright 2001
All Rights Reserved
Glenn Thomas LCSW
P.O. Box 937, Saratoga, CA 95071

ISBN 0-9711992-0-5

Book Editing by Tenaya Adams and Cyndy Thomas LCSW
Cover Design by Steven Adams and Cyndy Thomas LCSW
Book Layout by Steven Adams
Illustrations conceptualized by Glenn Thomas LCSW
Illustrations by Sean Adams

CONTENTS

This book is dedicated to my wife who is still my best friend, my co-therapist, and my inspiration after all these years.

INTRODUCTION

We hope this book reaches the widest audience possible.

You can read and use this book in one sitting.

We encourage you to explore its simplicity. The ideas present themselves quickly. Awareness grows slowly.

CHAPTER ONE: THE CLARITY CHART

Many of us learn visually.

We create a display on poster board for our clients to see every time they come in for counseling.

We call it the *"Clarity Chart."* We will call it just Chart for short.

The Chart changed the way we work with our clients.

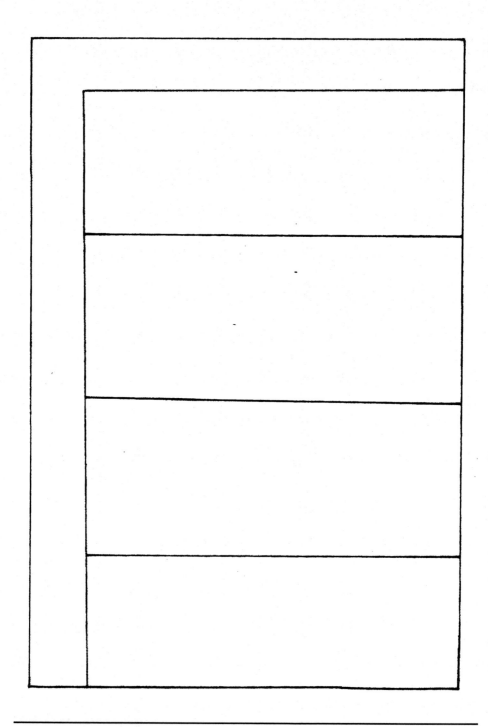

Let's start by making a Chart right now. Refer to the Chart on the previous page as we go through this exercise.

Please get a blank 8 ½ x 11 inch piece of paper. This chart will be your own Chart.

Draw a line to create a border on the left and top side of the blank page. Next draw three horizontal lines to create four separate sections.

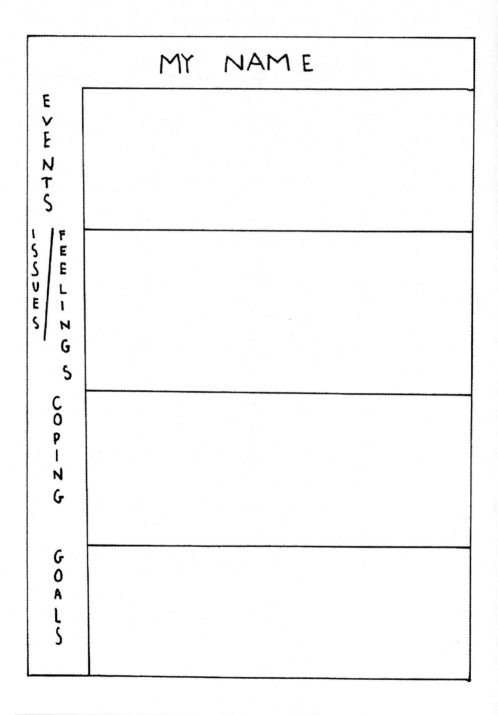

MY NAME

EVENTS

ISSUES / FEELINGS

COPING

GOALS

Please label the top border with your name.

Label the left top row border EVENTS, the next row ISSUES/FEELINGS, the next row COP-ING, and the bottom row GOALS.

Your Chart should look like the chart on the previous page.

You can put it aside for now. We'll get back to it later.

NAME

EVENTS / ISSUES

asdfgh lka ysh dfksha cuenos dliswdas sd wiur
d asd aserres sdoebb dsfdw p;wks shks
sd g gdfgds afkdpwqd sdposww er

FEELINGS

asdfgh lka ysh dfkshasdshfkas hdfg
d asd aserres sdoebb sdfsa sad euci

hdfsl, sdlkOe, asks, & asdslue

COPING

'kasdfgh lka ysh dfkshasdshfkas hdfg
d asd aserres sdoebb sdf
;lksdie qp ila cils fdshiqw adisiw iso
e wpofkdpwqd sdposwwer

GOALS

sadflksd poiw mdp lsise sp
a skdhive eecerssf sdaflksnw ooisf lislis eislas sdngxis
dsiw s awopro okpoke e;o sosee
sldsoiwe risofddo pwqin

We use standard white poster board 22 inches by 28 inches to make a Chart. We mark out the boards using felt pens.

We use different colors for Events, Issues, Feelings, Coping, and Goals so they stand out.

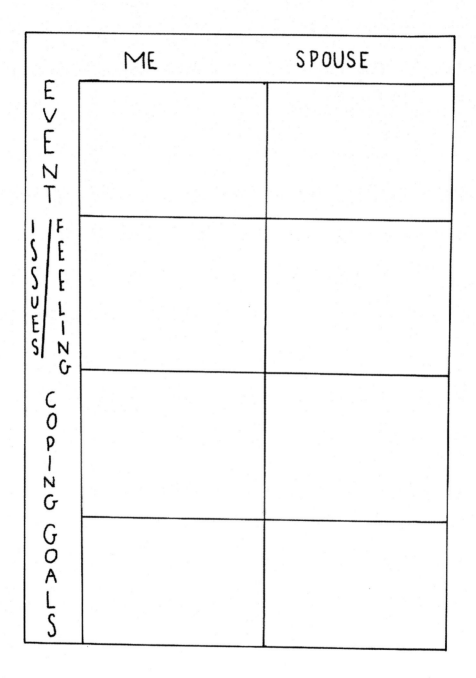

	ME	SPOUSE
EVENT		
ISSUES / FEELING		
COPING		
GOALS		

Look at the previous page if you want to make a couple's Chart.

Prepare it like an individual chart but draw a vertical line down the center of the four rows. Put your name and your spouse's or companion's name on top.

We work with many couples using the couple's Chart.

PAST

_____

PRESENT

_____

FUTURE

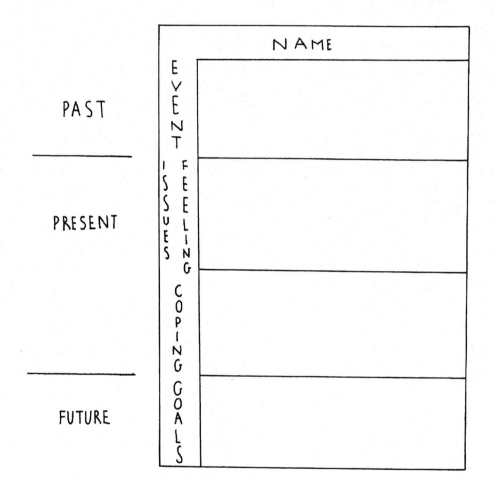

NAME

EVENT

ISSUES FEELING

COPING GOALS

The Chart gives us a **developmental** view.

Past: Events

Present: Issues and related Feelings and Coping with those Feelings.

Future: Goals

This display also provides a continuity of treatment.

During every treatment we refer to the client's Chart that we thumb tack to a cork board in our treatment room.

The Chart is our reference point. It shows us where we've been, where we are, and where we are going.

The Chart makes sense to us as therapists.

It is simple to explain and understand.

And more importantly, over the past thirteen years of using the Chart daily, it works!

The Chart works by heightening our aware-ness about the development of some of our dys-functional behaviors, especially unhealthy ways we cope.

Sometimes the wonderful experience of aware-ness, of how and why we have certain behav-iors, enables us to find understanding.

And from that understanding we desire change.

We often need a second ingredient to change: crisis. Crisis provides the push to lower our usual defenses and face what has always been there.

Crisis & Awareness

Change is painful and once we've crossed through it, wonderful!

Another way the Chart works is by focusing our desire for change into a forward direction: Goals.

So often an individual can gain awareness, but lack direction.

It's like raising the dust and watching it settle again.

If we decide to have Goals, we can find the tools to reach them.

We get these tools from friends, family, helpers, and therapists.

Like any instrument, the Chart is as good as the artisan using it.

The paint brush does not make the beginner painter a master; talent and maturation bring expertise.

Therapy novices will wield the Chart technically. Experienced therapists will orchestrate it using their orientation and years of practice.

The Chart is effective for only a segment of the population.

You must be cognitively mature, grounded in reality, and sophisticated enough to make sense of the Chart.

You must be healthy enough to view your dysfunction as a problem.

NAME

EVENTS
ISSUES
FEELINGS
COPING
GOALS

EMOTIONAL INJURIES

RESULTING ISSUES

FEELINGS

COPING BEHAVIORS WITH STRONG FEELINGS

PERSONAL GOALS FOR CHANGE

Now we'll give you the overall big picture:

1. When we view a Clarity Chart, we see our important emotionally injurious **Events**.

2. We see our **Issues** and underlying **Feelings** arising from these Events.

3. We observe our **Coping** behaviors with which we try to manage the uncomfortable **Feelings** related to these Issues.

4. We record our personal **Goals** (often the goals arise from changing unhealthy coping) to map our direction.

5. Finally, we get the tools to make the changes we want.

6. Viewing the Chart every session provides continuity of treatment and enhances awareness of ourselves.

Now you have an idea where we are heading. Keep reading and follow along the trail of this book. We'll make many scenic stops along the way to help clarify the Chart.

Part of the scenery will be an example session where we develop a couple's Chart.

Scenes of four chart examples & explanations will help your understanding of the Chart.

Now a closer look at the four sections of the Chart.

1. Events
2. Issue/Feelings
3. Coping
4. Goals

The **Events** we write on the Chart are usually emotional injuries that result in **Issues**.

We can't go through life without some emotional injuries.

However, depending on their severity, emotional injuries can affect us for a lifetime.

We might go through life emotionally wounded.

We can lessen the damage of the Event and promote healing by increasing our awareness of the Event and how it has affected us.

Aware action sure beats unconscious reaction.

EVENTS Examples:

Parents divorce

Hospitalization

Emotional abuse

Physical abuse

Racism

Betrayal by spouse, parent, or friend

Mentally ill parent

Victim or witness to a crime

Death of a parent, spouse, or sibling

Sexual abuse

Own divorce

Over controlling parent

Random catastrophic event

Depressed parent

Angry parent

Sibling incest

Poverty

Lack of parental supervision

Birth order

Failed career

Substance abuse

Workaholic parent or spouse

Deprived of education

Abandoned by spouse, parent, or friend

Alcoholic parent

Loss of best friend

Bigotry

Neglect

Born with organic problems

Victim of war

Sudden loss of choices

Loss of future dreams

Environmental catastrophe

Many other kinds of emotionally injurious events

The previous page shows a partial list of common emotional injuries.

If you have experienced any of these Events, please include them in the chart you made earlier, or use a blank Chart in the back of the book. Please write them in the Event row.

If we have not listed Events in your life that were emotional injuries, please write the Events on your Chart.

CHAPTER THREE: ISSUES

Issues run through our lives with themes arising from our past Events.

Issues echo in our experiences in an effort to guard us from uncomfortable Feelings.

We sensitize ourselves and hide our awareness of Issues in an effort to protect ourselves from pain.

Issues are like a road of the unconscious.

We've traveled this road before. We have the same kinds of problems over and over again.

The content may be different, but the processes, or patterns, are the same.

EVENT: ISSUE(S)

Death of Parent: **Abandonment**
Sibling Favored: **Fairness**
Poverty: **Security**
Alcoholic Parents: **Control, Trust, Unimportance, Safety**
Being Adopted: **Attachment**
Abandoned by Spouse, Parent or Friend: **Trust, Abandonment**
Ignored by Parent: **Unimportance**
Critical Parent: **Adequacy**
Abused: **Trust, Safety**
Undependable Parent: **Trust**
Parental Unacceptance: **Belonging, Trust**
Out of Control Parent: **Control vs Out of Control**
Conditional Love: **Perfectionism, Control**
Withdrawn Mom or Dad: **Dependency**
Divorce: **Abandonment**
Mentally Ill Parent: **Safety, Trust**
Betrayal by Spouse, Parent or Friend: **Trust, Attachment**
Lack of Parental Supervision: **Dependency, Trust**
Victim or Witness of a Crime or   Violence: **Safety, Trust, Control**
Loss of Future Dreams: **Attachment**
Racism & Bigotry: **Trust, Safety**
Random Catastrophic Event: **Safety, Control**

The previous page shows a partial list of common Issues associated with certain Events.

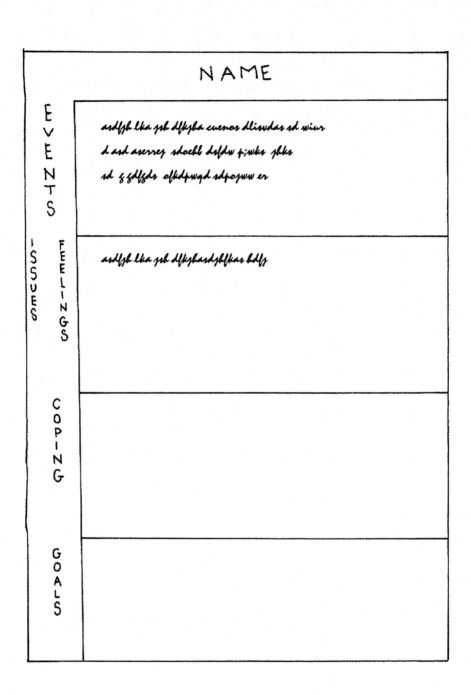

As an example, let's choose "I grew up with an alcoholic father" as one of our Events.

I became the "Lost child." I coped by disappearing and withdrawing in a family full of drama and conflict. I got lost and lost myself in the crisis.

Out of this Event or series of the same Event I developed the Issue "I am Unimportant."

We now have an Event and Issue to place in an example Chart on the previous page.

Remember, Issues lose their unconscious control over us when we become aware of them.

Then our dysfunctional behaviors make sense to us and form the content of our process.

Awareness is like fog rolling back, another Vista Point in our lives.

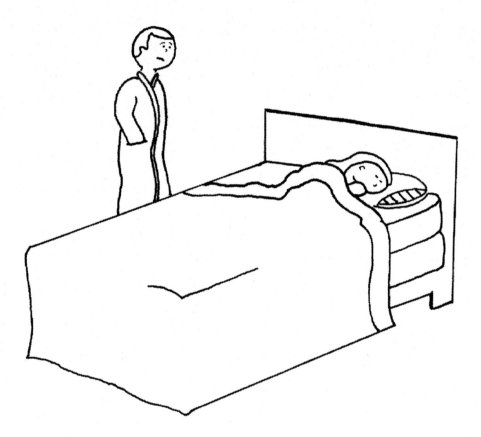

Let's look at some possible content behaviors of the Issue "I am Unimportant."

I went to bed early. When I woke up in the morning, I realized my wife had stayed up late working on a report. She hadn't bothered to wake me up for some romance.

I feel very HURT and ANGRY. I bury my feelings and won't talk to her.

I get to the office and see some co-workers going off to lunch.

Even though I am not close to them, I feel HURT and SAD at not having been invited.

I stay inside and hide in my work.

I hear a co-worker deservedly got a promotion.

I feel HURT and SAD, even though I admire this person's work.

I find it hard to compliment this individual and I keep quiet.

I come home from work and see my wife. She doesn't kiss me right away.

My feelings get HURT. I don't tell her.

I act a little quiet and withdrawn.

My daughter comes into the room and asks only her mother a question and leaves.

I feel HURT and ANGRY.

I go and watch some TV.

" I AM UNIMPORTANT "

All these situations revolve around one Issue, one process: "I am unimportant."

Another person without the Issue "I am unimportant" might experience some of the feelings, but not as strongly.

But it is a strong Issue for me. The Issue arises from an emotionally injurious Event, the "lost child" in an alcoholic family.

Did you ever interact with someone who seemed overly sensitive about something?

Maybe he or she was re-experiencing the strong Emotions under an Issue.

NAME

EVENTS

ISSUES

FEELINGS

asdfjh lka jsh dfkjha cuenos dliswdas sd wiur

d asd aserres sdoehb dsfdw p;wks jhks

sd g gdlfgds ofkdpwqd sdpojww er

asdfjh lka jsh dfkjhasdjshfkas hdfs

d asd aserres sdoehb sdlfsa sad euei

hdfjl, sdlkOe, asks, & asdslue

COPING

GOALS

Please get your Chart out again.

Looking at the Events you wrote on your personal Chart, choose from among the Issues in the Common Events/Issues list on page 44 that seem to fit you.

If you can think of other Issues that do not appear listed, please use them.

Please write the Issues down in the Issues section of your Chart. Leave some space to write under each Issue.

CHAPTER FOUR: FEELINGS

Under every Issue is one or more Feelings.

When I am re-experiencing an Issue, I experience a Feeling or Feelings arising from that Issue.

SCARED

HAPPY

EXCITED

HURT

ANGRY

SAD

We simplify the identification of Feelings under an Issue by only using six different Feelings:

Scared
Happy
Excited
Hurt
Angry
Sad

Please notice the acronym of these feelings is **"SHE HAS."**

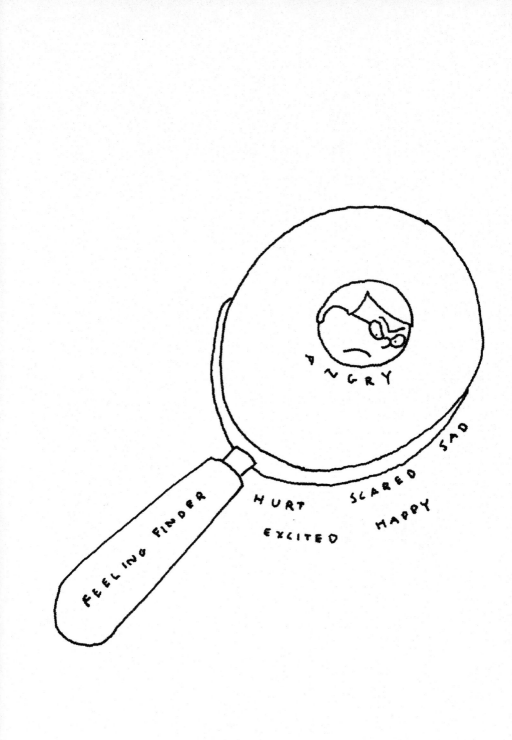

Many of our Feelings fit one of the six Feelings:

1   **Scared** = worried, concerned, anxious, nervous, uptight, shaky, fearful, terrified

2   **Happy** = elated, glad, up, content, peaceful, mellow

3   **Excited** = turned on, ecstatic, aflame, energetic, high spirited, enthusiastic, lively, hyper

4   **Hurt** = betrayed, stepped on, disappointed, crushed, devastated, painful, embarrassed, injured, torn up, in pieces

5   **Angry** = mad, upset, bored, irritated, furious, annoyed, pissed off, perturbed, enraged, livid, fuming, burning, boiling

6   **Sad** = bummed out, down, blue, melancholy, sorrowful, heavy, despair, tearful, burdened, low, awful

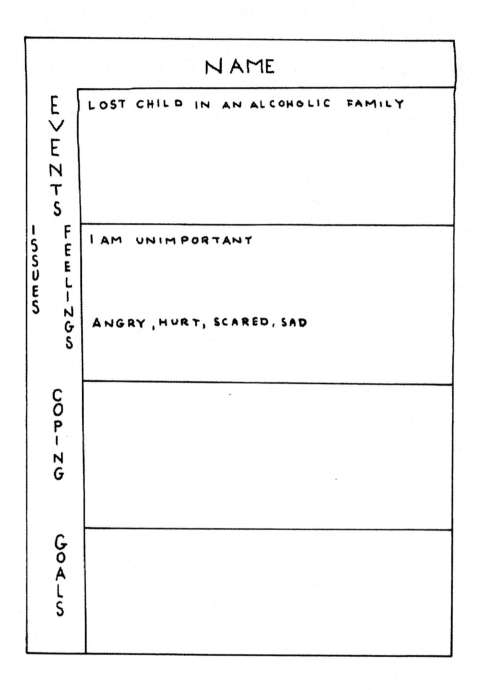

NAME

EVENTS

ISSUES

FEELINGS

LOST CHILD IN AN ALCOHOLIC FAMILY

I AM UNIMPORTANT

ANGRY, HURT, SCARED, SAD

COPING

GOALS

Let's use our original Issue, "I am unimportant."

We could put the Feelings "Angry, Sad, Hurt, and Scared" under the Issue.

When I am experiencing being unimportant, I feel Angry, Sad, Hurt, and Scared at different times.

We can see Feelings in our example Chart now on the previous page.

NAME

EVENTS

asdfgh lka psh dfkgha cuenor dliswdas sd wiur
d asd aserrez sdoehb dsfdw p;wks ghks
sd g sdfgds ofkdpwqd sdpopww er

ISSUES

FEELINGS

asdfgh lka psh dfkghasdghfkar bdfg
d asd aserrez sdoehb sdfpa sad cuei dwakp

kdfpl, sdlkOe, asky, & asdslue
sdf; lksd s

COPING

GOALS

Please get your Chart out again.

Under the Issues part of your Chart, write down which of the six Feelings you get when you are experiencing your Issues.

Please look at the list of the six Feelings on page 69.

Please use a different color to write the Feelings right under the Issue.

You can have more than one Feeling under an Issue.

Take your time identifying your Feelings.

Sometimes we are unaware that we feel scared when we are about to enter an Issue-laden situation.

Next on the Chart is Coping.

Coping is how we handle the Feeling that arises out of the Issue.

CHAPTER FIVE: COPING

What we do with Feelings is extremely important.

There are healthy and unhealthy ways of Coping with Feelings.

Sometimes unhealthy ways of Coping with Feelings make problems in our lives and lead us to treatment.

We'll use one of our example **Issues,** "I am unimportant" with the underlying **Feelings** of Anger, Hurt, Sad and Scared:

Issue/Event: "I went to bed early. When I woke up in the morning, I realized my wife had stayed up late working on a report. She hadn't bothered to wake me up for some romance."

Feeling: I feel very HURT and ANGRY. I bury my Feelings and won't talk to her.

How I **Coped** with my Feelings: I stuffed them inside. I didn't give them directly to my wife by talking to her.

I stayed hidden (the lost child) by avoiding conflict. This hiding may have worked for me as a child Coping with the dysfunction in my family, but it doesn't work now.

Common ways of Coping are:

Avoiding
Taking feelings out on others
Denying
Overeating
Minimizing
Drinking alcohol
Overworking
Talking a lot
Rationalizing
Raging
Blaming
Externalizing
Working harder, faster
Abusing drugs
Abusing sex
Being a rescuer
Hiding
Not letting it get to me
Acting like it didn't happen
Not talking about it
Staying at work
Overexercising
Abusing self/others
Driving fast
Repressing
Scapegoating
Not trusting
Not feeling

Feeling numb
Talking behind their backs
Suffering in silence
Being a victim
Sweeping problems under the carpet
Feeling sorry for myself
Seeking revenge
Being passive aggressive
Controlling others
Belittling and shaming
Nagging
Playing head games
Punishing
Manipulating
Zoning out with something
Ignoring feelings
Believing it will get better
Avoiding confrontation
Cleaning things
Trips
Doing yard work
Shopping
Getting distracted
Talking to myself
Escaping through Entertainment

On the previous page you will find common examples of the many ways we Cope with strong Feelings.

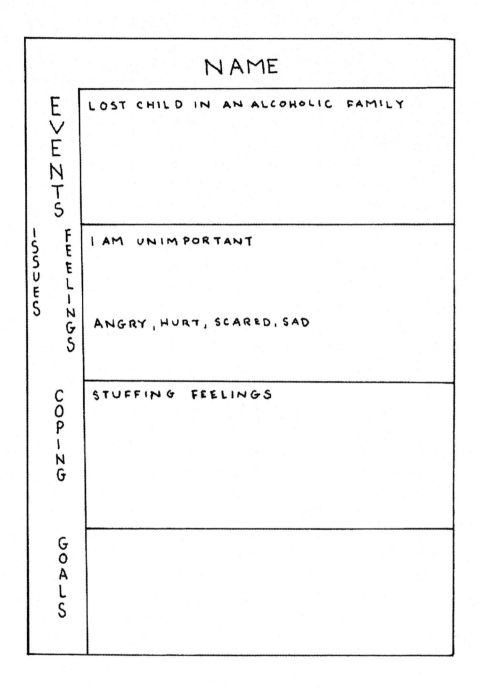

NAME

EVENTS · ISSUES

LOST CHILD IN AN ALCOHOLIC FAMILY

FEELINGS

I AM UNIMPORTANT

ANGRY, HURT, SCARED, SAD

COPING

STUFFING FEELINGS

GOALS

So now we see on our example Chart:

Event: Lost child in an alcoholic family

Issue/Feelings: Unimportant/Hurt, Angry, Scared, Sad

Coping: Stuffing Feelings and avoiding

I now understand why I am so sensitive to many situations that bring up my Issue of "I am Unimportant." I have increased my level of awareness.

I know I developed my Issue of "I am Unimportant" from my Event of being a child in an alcoholic family.

I know when I am experiencing being "Unimportant" I feel at different times angry, sad, hurt, and scared.

I know what I do with those Feelings. I typically avoid and stuff them inside me.

I write these pieces of awareness on my Chart to reflect on them now and refer to them later.

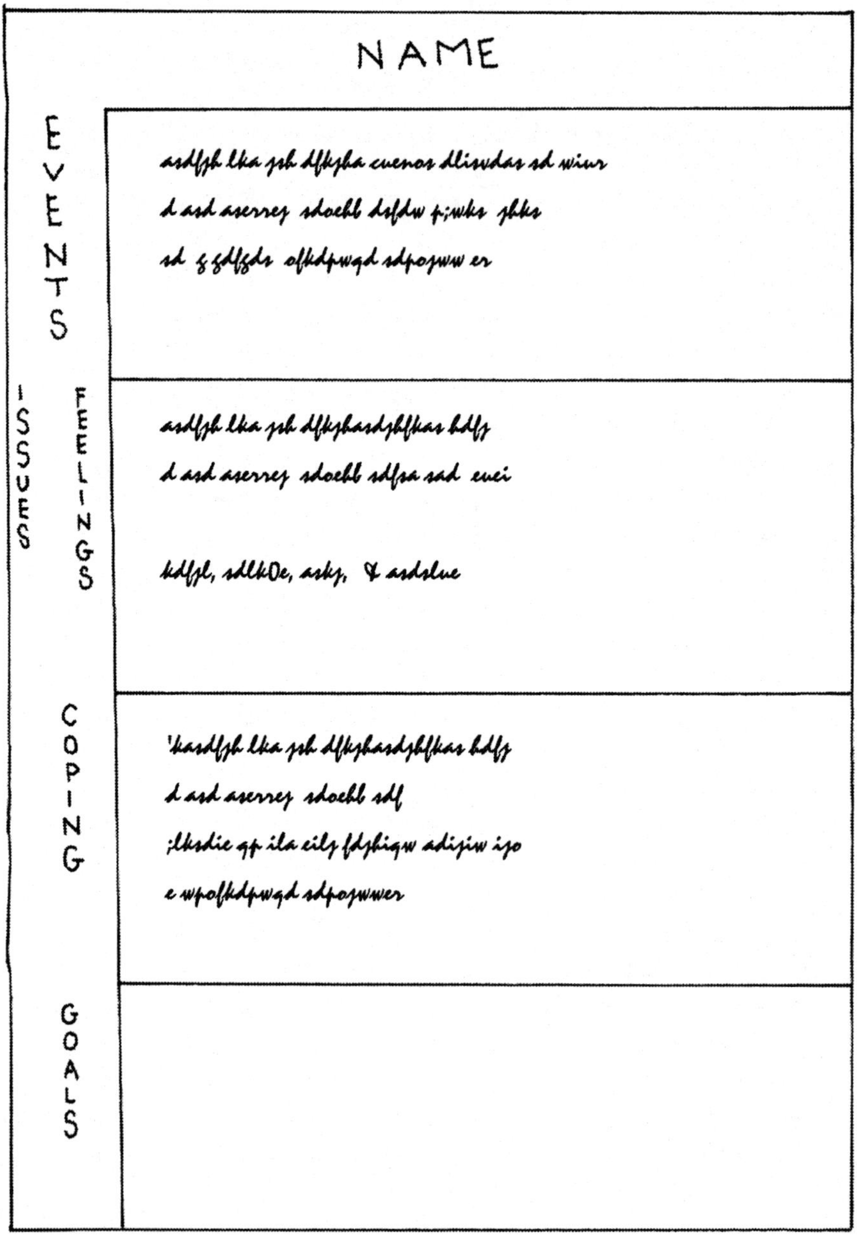

NAME	
EVENTS	asdfjh lka jsh dfkjha cuenos dlisudas sd wiur d asd aserres sdoehb dsfdw p;wks jhks sd g gdfgds ofkdpwqd sdpojww er
FEELINGS	asdfjh lka jsh dfkjhasdjshfkas bdfj d asd aserres sdoehb sdfpa sad euei kdfjl, sdlkOe, asks, & asdslue
COPING	'kasdfjh lka jsh dfkjhasdjshfkas bdfj d asd aserres sdoehb sdf ;lksdie qp ila cils fdshiqw adijiw ijo e wpofkdpwqd sdpojwwer
GOALS	

(left margin label: ISSUES)

Please go back and look at your own Chart. Look at your Issues and the Feelings under them.

Under the Coping section of your Chart, please write down what you do with those Feelings.

Look at page 80 for the list of common ways of Coping.

Important hint:

What would other people see you doing or not doing that would show them you are experiencing these Feelings?

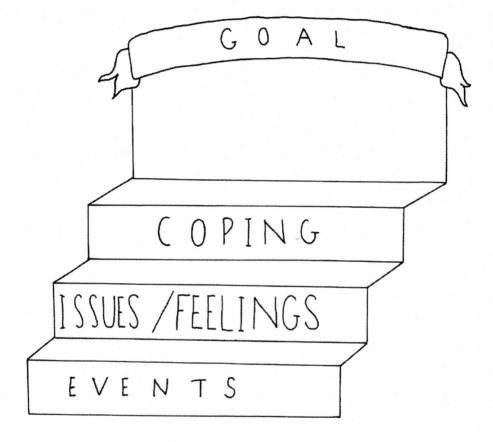

Gradually with practice we become aware when we are swimming in an Issue and using unhealthy Coping to deal with our Feelings.

We cannot make the Event go away. We cannot make the Issue disappear. We're not likely to completely get rid of our Feelings under the Issue.

However, we can behave differently.

That choice to Cope (behave) differently becomes a Goal. Goals are the last stage in the Chart.

We work toward Goals.

Goals are future directed.

Chart Goals usually come from changing a way we Cope.

When we're aware of how we react to uncomfortable Feelings with unhealthy behavior, we're ready for Goals.

Goals are extremely important for change.

If our Goals are merely the therapist's Goals or a spouse's Goals, we are setting ourselves up for certain failure.

And even worse, we are not empowering ourselves.

Sometimes therapists charge ahead on our path. They don't get the personal commitment from us to own the path (Goal) without persuasion.

Therapists may get angry at us for not moving toward the Goal.

It's the therapists' mistake in therapeutic pacing.

Don't race, pace!

NAME

EVENTS

asdfgh lka gsh dfkgha cuenos dliswdas sd wiur
d asd aserrey sdoehb dsfdw q;whs ghhs
sd g gdfgds ofkdpwqd sdposww er

ISSUES

FEELINGS

asdfgh lka gsh dfkghasdghfkas hdfg
d asd aserrey sdoehb sdfsa sad cuei

hdfgl, sdlkOe, asky, & asdslue

COPING

'kasdfgh lka gsh dfkghasdghfkas hdfg
d asd aserrey sdoehb sdf
;lksdie gp ila cily fdghigw adigiw igo
e wpofkdpwqd sdposwwer

GOALS

The Chart is filled out in developmental order, from top to bottom.

Usually the Events, Issues, Feelings, and Coping are filled in, until most of them are written on the chart. This leaves only the Goals to be finished.

Weeks can go by before we are willing to venture onto Goals.

This is very apparent when using the Chart with couples.

Usually one person in the couple moves more quickly toward Goals.

We must have a certain level of trust, self-esteem, and ego strength to risk personal Goals.

Therapeutic pacing is important so a therapist doesn't scare the client away.

Don't pry defenses away!

A trusting therapeutic relationship helps lower defenses.

In the example Issue "I am Unimportant," my Coping was to "stuff my feelings and avoid confrontation."

Stuffing is a problem for me. I appear withdrawn, cold, and my feelings aren't heard by my wife.

I avoid a possible solution to the problem.

I can decide to make my Goal: "Be direct and current with my Feelings."

I get this Goal by looking in the Coping section of my Chart.

I notice how I usually Cope in an unhealthy way, and I decide to make my Coping behavior positive.

I now have a direction. I can achieve this Goal if I decide to make the Goal.

It's my OWN decision.

I can change.

I must be willing to experience very uncomfortable Feelings to meet my Goals.

This is the price I pay to be healthy.

I must now walk directly into the Feelings I once avoided.

Common Goals are:

Express my Feelings
Say I'm sorry
End my sarcasm
Be positive
Get help with my depression
Be able to confront others
Give more compliments
Make requests, not demands
Be more playful with spouse
Pay more attention to my spouse
Lower my defensive wall
Work as a team
Refrain from hitting in our home
Be current & direct with my feelings
Say appreciative words
Get help with my abuse
Be more sympathetic
Praise others more
Talk more openly
Give hugs to my family
Spend more time w/ spouse
Accept compliments
Stand up to others
Communicate more
Give more attention to my spouse
Praise others' efforts
Share non-judging Feelings
Say what I mean
Mean what I say
Find more humor in life
Be more tolerant of differences
Be less sarcastic
Say no and mean it
Express hurt Feelings
Be less controlling
Have greater self-awareness
Be more sensitive w/ my remarks
Be more connected to Feelings
Allow spouse to meet my needs
Set realistic expectations
Deal with my own guilt
Be honest with myself
Think of consequences
Don't worry about what others think
Just do it
Get help with my anxiety

Use eye contact
Read books on co-dependency
Go back to school
Control my shopping
Control my addictions
Don't leave. Instead stay and connect
Risk not being perfect
Be more spontaneous
Get help with my anger
Risk rejection
Initiate lovemaking
Be less critical
Be more trusting
Open up about my past
Share goals and future plans
Be more enthusiastic
Be flexible socially
Be more agreeable
Stop saying "never and always"
Stop swearing
Use fewer explanations
Stop trying to fix everybody
Stop being abusive
Spend one on one quality time w/ kids
Get physically fit
Take more interest in others
Take control of my anger
Make plans for the weekend
Stop bullying others
Stay present, don't withdraw
Give up my addictions
Show respect for others
Stay, don't run
Take a time out before I blow up
Come out of hiding
Try new things
Don't put others down
Be less defensive
Write down feelings
Stay clean and sober
Know, say, get
Go out with spouse once a week
Be more aware of my sexuality
Don't threaten divorce
Empathize with others more
Keep my volume down
Let my spouse calm down
Stop putting myself down
Develop same age friendships

On the previous page you will find common examples of Goals.

One of the most powerful moments in the mid-point of therapy comes when the therapist asks the client,

"Is this behavior something you want to change?"

Being asked this question helps us own our problem behavior and step toward our Goals.

"IM READY"

Before asking this question, the therapist must be sure that we are aware of our problem behavior.

PERSONAL
GROWTH

We get Tools to change from our family, friends, self-help groups, or therapists.

NAME

EVENTS	
	LOST CHILD IN AN ALCOHOLIC FAMILY
ISSUES / FEELINGS	I AM UNIMPORTANT ANGRY, HURT, SCARED, SAD
COPING	STUFFING FEELINGS
GOALS	BE CURRENT AND DIRECT WITH MY FEELINGS

Event: Lost child in an alcoholic family

Issue/Feelings: I am unimportant/Anger, Hurt, Scared, Sad

Coping: Stuff my Feelings & avoid

Goal: Be current and direct with my Feelings

Remember, I may have many Issues. We have only one Issue listed in our example Chart.

Now, please go to your own Chart and look at how you Cope with the uncomfortable Feelings under your Issues.

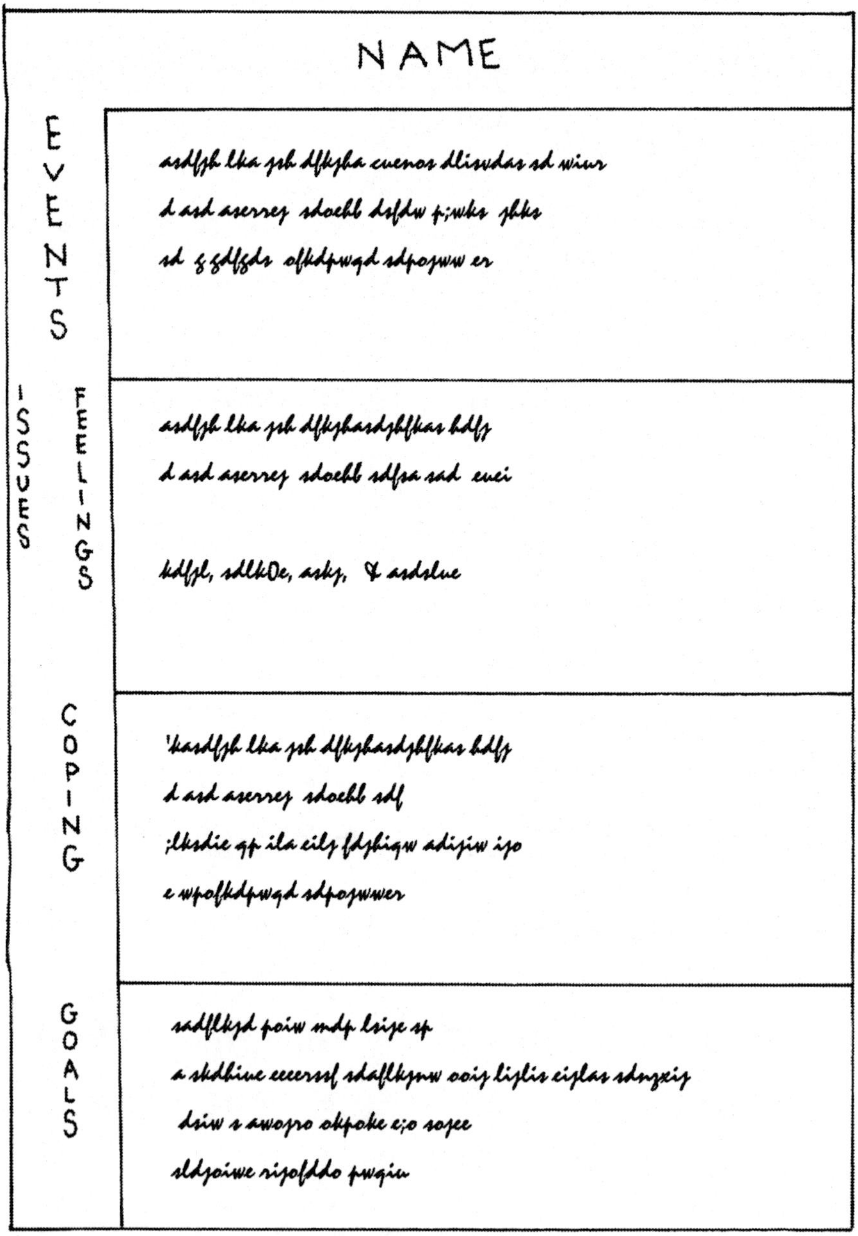
NAME
EVENTS
ISSUES
FEELINGS
COPING
GOALS

Look to see if any of the ways you Cope pose a problem. If your Coping behavior creates difficulty, decide if you want to change it.

Then write down the changed Coping as a Goal in the Goal section of your personal Chart.

PERSONAL
GROWTH

Most people stop at this point. A lot of us know what we should do to be healthier.

We should give up an addiction, stand up to some-body, take a risk, or maybe try something we fear.

A crisis sometimes pushes us to take that first step. We don't have to wait for a crisis. We don't have to wait until our backs are to the wall.

If we can move through what is painful, we can experience something wonderful.

From our intentions, we move to action. We pick up Tools and make a different life for ourselves and for our families.

But sometimes awareness is like a very slow-growing flower.

You don't have to wait another moment of your life. Go out and get the Tools you need to change. Do it now.

Let's look at some example Tools: anger management, family therapy, marriage counseling, Alcoholics Anonymous, therapeutic groups, Jungian analysis, behavior modification, individual therapy, financial advice, Gestalt therapy, Rational-Emotive therapy, stress management, Narcotics Anonymous, brief therapy, inpatient alcohol programs, fitness programs, bio-feedback, support groups, churches, workshops, retreats, shelters, legal advice, self defense, education, parenting classes, public speaking classes, Overeaters Anonymous, self awareness classes and many others.

You can get these Tools by talking to family, friends, helpers, and trained professionals.

Sometimes we need help and encouragement from people we trust to make courageous decisions.

We can change our can'ts to cans, our impossibilities to possibilities, our walls to doors opening out to ourselves.

We are worth discovering and loving.

We add healthy Coping to the Chart toward the end of treatment.

Why toward the end? Some of us have powerful defenses.

We see ourselves as having no problems. This behavior reflects our strong Issues of perfection and control. We are unwilling to be vulnerable to an emotional attack.

Preparing a Chart in the middle work of treatment focuses on emotional injuries and helps us confront our denial.

We encourage low self-esteem clients, without perfection and control issues, to highlight areas of health on the Chart.

We add these strengths to the Chart only when we are ready to accept them.

We suggest you rework your Chart after you read the example charts and session in the following chapters.

Your understanding of the Chart should deepen by the end of the book. Your reworked chart will reflect this new-found understanding.

We suggest you seek a trained professional for Tools and in-depth understanding.

Ask a friend or doctor for a referral to an experienced Family and Child Counselor, Clinical Social Worker, Psychologist, or Psychiatrist who can deepen your work with the Chart.

CHAPTER SEVEN:
CLARITY CHART EXAMPLES

Four example Charts follow. A short explanation accompanies each chart.

		Kerry	Matt

I S S U E S	**E V E N T S**	family of origin
		       kept feelings
		       inside
		
		Abusive relationships
		
		Divorce
			mom suicide attempt
			Dad left
			little memory before six
			Divorce
			
			Caretaker

	F E E L I N G S	need for
		Connection + emotion
		Perfection - scared
		Abandonment - attachment
		hurt, scared < flight
		            fight
		  criticized
		unimportant / ignored
		    sad angry
		uninformed - mad, hurt
			Abandonment
			scared < fight hurt
			       flight sad
			         not cared for
			Taking care of others in
			crisis / excited, scared
			out of control unfair
			  scared anger, hurt
			Safety
			  scared

	C O P I N G	close up - quiet watch TV alot eat chocolate Talk to cats "not let anyone inside" Venting through moods	Doing activity by myself puts hands over eyes when I don't like to deal with venting w/ moody put feeling in corner
	G O A L S	write feelings down Open up and be direct Take more care of Matt acknowledge efforts Relax	write feelings down Don't throw things not throw "it" in Kerrys face when I feel criticized express the hurt Know, say, get

1. KERRY & MATT

Kerry and Matt want couples' counseling. They are not married at the time of the first session. They fight all the time and have difficulty communicating. Their fights last for days. During the middle phase of treatment, Kerry and Matt get married.

	Kerry	Matt

E V E N T S	family of origin
	    kept feelings
	    inside
	
	Abusive relationships
	
	Divorce
		mom suicide attempt
		Dad left
		little memory before six
		Divorce
		
		Caretaker

EVENTS:

Kerry learned as a child to keep her feelings inside. At 9, her parents divorced. Her brother physically abused her as a child. Her worst memory involved her brother threatening to injure her. Her father did nothing to protect her. Kerry trusted no one and took care of herself.

Matt's mother attempted suicide when Matt was 9 years old. His biological father abandoned the family when Matt was 12. Matt remembers taking care of his mother when he was only 13 by cooking and cleaning and watching his little sister and brother.

		Kerry	Matt
I S S U E S	F E E L I N G S	need for Connection + emotion Perfection - scared Abandonment - attachment hurt, scared ⟨ flight / fight criticized unimportant / ignored sad angry uninformed - mad, hurt	Abandonment hurt scared ⟨ fight / flight sad not cared for Taking care of others in crisis / excited, scared out of control unfair scared anger, hurt Safety scared

ISSUES/FEELINGS:

Kerry has a strong need to connect to someone. Abandonment is a keen Issue for Kerry since her parents left her emotionally. Similarly, unimportance is a sensitive area for her. She develops perfectionism as a way to avoid punishment and not give anyone reason to leave her. Criticism, a key Issue that causes scared feelings and anger, arises from her brother's critical abuse of her. Kerry becomes mad and hurt when uninformed by others, a result of needing to know what to be prepared for in her family of origin.

Matt has similar issues of abandonment coming from his father's leaving the family and his mother's withdrawal into depression. He has a strong need to be cared for, even while representing the caretaker in the relationship. Because his mother was out of control, Matt is afraid of situations where he has no control. He perceives his entire childhood experience as unfair.

	Kerry	Matt
C O P I N G	close up - quiet watch TV alot eat chocolate Talk to cats "not let anyone inside" venting through moods	Doing activity by myself puts hands over eyes when I dont like to deal with venting w/ moody put feeling in corner

COPING:

To Cope with her Feelings, Kerry withdraws into TV, eats sweets, plays with her cats, and does not let anyone get too close to her. She expresses anger even when she feels hurt, sad, or scared. She acts moody and vents on Matt. She needs him to take care of her and attach to her. She isn't used to caring for anyone else. Matt appears safe to Kerry because of his strong caretaker behaviors.

Matt, on the other hand, feels compelled to take care of Kerry, even though he resents her lack of care for him. He sees himself as a victim. Matt uses work outside to escape the hurt of emotional distance. He tends to projects and work around the house. Matt experiences himself as alone, like when he was a young caretaker.

	Kerry	Matt
G O A L S	write feelings down Open up and be direct Take more care of Matt acknowledge efforts Relax	write feelings down Dont throw things not throw "it" in Kerrys face when I feel criticized express the hurt Know, say, get

GOALS:

Kerry decides to write down her feelings for Matt to read. She finds this form of expression easier than talking. By writing down her feelings, she stops being moody. After she gets used to expressing her feelings in writing, Kerry finds she can open up verbally to Matt.

Matt writes his feelings to Kerry. This writing works well for both of them. It allows them to think more about what they really want to communicate to each other. The writing turns to love letters. Matt and Kerry continue to have some difficulties, but the writing helps them express their feelings for each other.

		Anne	Todd
E V E N T S		Moms miscarriage (age 6) little girl, 3 yrs old, left	Divorce of parents (age 9) Hard to please Dad
I S S U E S	**F E E L I N G S**	Trust abandohment Acceptance not wanted HURT Defiant to change Conflict hurt Perfection	Jealousy Rejection, anger, hurt feeling wanted, desired happy, excited UNFAIR Sad need appreciation
	C O P I N G	Taking care of others not myself quiet clean Avoid Express w/ writting	express feelings throw pillow leave Gets loud
	G O A L S	Say "Thank you" Recognize the need of Tod Accept my diabetes Just say "no" Acknowledge Tods feelings "Im sorry"	Aware of coping walk- cool down PATIENT Change critical tone

2. ANNE & TODD

Anne was in individual treatment with us off and on for two years in an attempt to leave a relationship she felt guilty leaving. Anne ended treatment for another two years, met a young man, and fell in love. She wanted them to come in for couples' counseling to lessen their fighting. They attended counseling for about four months. Anne and Todd returned for more treatment six months later and are now doing well.

	Anne	Todd
E V E N T S	Moms miscarriage (age 6) little girl, 3 yrs old, left	Divorce of parents (age 9) Hard to please Dad

EVENTS:

Anne grew up in a family where her father took a traveling salesman job. He was gone three weeks out of every month. Her mother had a miscarriage when Anne was six years old. Anne asked her mother when she was going to see the new baby, and her mother ran into her bedroom crying. Anne's father took her into the family room and told her not to bother her mother since her mother had just lost the baby. Anne never bothered her mother again. Instead, Anne was over involved with her father and grew up spoiled. Anne developed diabetes towards the end of counseling.

Todd's parents divorced when he was nine. His father was an unemployed alcoholic who had little praise for his son. Todd assumed the role of man of the household. He got a paper route and helped support his mother with the little money he earned.

		Anne	Todd
I S S U E S	F E E L I N G S	Trust abandonment Acceptance not wanted HURT Defiant to change Conflict hurt Perfection	Jealousy Rejection, anger, hurt feeling wanted, desired happy, excited UNFAIR Sad need appreciation

ISSUES/FEELINGS:

Anne experiences Issues of trust and abandonment as a result of her withdrawal from her depressed and absent mother. Anne becomes very sensitive to conflict and any family disturbance. She develops the Issue of perfection to give no one reason to leave her. She becomes very leery of change.

Todd experiences Issues of feeling unwanted and abandoned. Control and caretaking become sensitive Issues for Todd.

	Anne	Todd
C O P I N G	Taking care of others not my self quiet clean Avoid Express w/ writting	express feelings throw pillow leave Gets loud

COPING:

Anne becomes a caretaker to make sure everyone around her is happy with her. She avoids situations where Issues of trust and abandonment might arise. She occasionally writes for expression. She feels happiest when she experiences being spoiled.

Todd gets angry and loud. When he feels overwhelmed, he leaves. He's afraid he will get out-of-hand. He throws things. He appears to express anger in unhealthy ways: when he feels sad, he expresses anger; when he feels scared, he expresses anger; when he feels hurt, he expresses anger.

	Anne	Todd
G O A L S	Say "Thank you" Recognize the need of Tod Accept my diabetes Just say "no" Acknowledge Tods feelings "Im sorry"	Aware of coping walk- cool down PATIENT Change critical tone

GOALS:

Anne recognizes Todd's needs as genuine and stops relating to him like a father figure. She stops avoiding conflict and says "yes" when she means yes and "no" when she means no. She becomes more vulnerable to Todd by thanking him for his kind deeds. She becomes less perfect by saying "sorry" when she is at fault.

Todd becomes aware of his intense anger and out-of-control behavior. He owns his problem of impatience and criticism of Anne. He learns anger management techniques and agrees to take walks to calm down.

		Donna	Brad
E V E N T S		Parents divorced (age 8 lived at home until age 23 mom died Donna 29 Birth of Tim (trauma) health unstable at times	Abuse by Dad (early child hood 7-15) separeted from mom Parented by sister Death of step dad Brad 28 almost lost Donna
I S S U E S	**F E E L I N G S**	Responsibility Independent Dependent anger (at self) Guilt wanted, needed vs. unneeded, reject Sad, hurt, angry	Abandonment loss vs. attach Fear, anger, hurt control / out of control Anger, fear
	C O P I N G	quiet channel surfing fluff pillows, bang on garage fridge not stick up for myself avoid mental hurt little depressed communication	Reassume myself Avoid - walk away from it Blaming shaming Projected voice Stone cold. faced "get the deck of cards together. put a rubber band on them"
	G O A L S	Be more open Be healty	Be more trusting Be more open Be aware of feelings when i relax

3. DONNA & BRAD

Donna and Brad came to us after Donna had slept on the couch for two years. They had developed a style of avoidance. They had sex only twice a year. Donna started going out with her closest single girlfriend. We saw Donna and Brad in treatment for four months. Their sex life greatly improved after they trusted each other with their feelings and shared their lives with each other.

	Donna	Brad

E
V
E
N
T
S
	Parents divorced (age 8
	lived at home until
	    age 23
	mom died Donna 29
	
	Birth of Tim (trauma)
	health unstable at
	times
		Abuse by Dad (early
		    childhood 7-15)
		separeted from mom
		Parented by sister
		Death of step dad
		    Brad 28
		
		almost lost Donna

EVENTS:

Donna's parents divorced when she was eight years old. The youngest child, Donna continued to live at home with her mother until she was twenty-three. Donna became very depressed when her mother died four years ago. Her son Tim was born shortly after her mother's death. Donna almost died from medical complications after giving birth to Tim. Her health is very unstable due to immune problems.

Brad was severely abused by his biological father from age seven to fifteen. Brad's father kidnapped him from his mother at age five and Brad did not see her again until age eighteen. Separated from his mother, Brad was raised by his older sister. At age eighteen he went to live with his mother and stepfather, whom he learned to love. The death of his stepdad when Brad was twenty-eight was devastating. Brad experienced trauma due to his wife's brush with death shortly after the birth of their son.

		Donna	Brad
I S S U E S	F E E L I N G S	Responsibility Independent Dependent anger (at self) Guilt wanted, needed vs. unneeded, reject Sad, hurt, angry	Abandonment loss vs. attach Fear, anger, hurt control / out of control Anger, fear

ISSUES/FEELINGS:

Donna develops Issues around responsibility and dependency. During her developmental years, Donna struggled between her desire for independence and her unmet dependency needs. She feels anger toward herself when she experiences dependency Issues with her husband. She watched her mother suffer from her attachment to her verbally abusive father. Deep down, Donna feels responsible for her parents' divorce. She thinks that if she had been a better daughter, mom and dad wouldn't have divorced. Issues of being wanted and needed come from the divorce and are heightened by the death of her mother.

Brad develops extreme Issues of abandonment and attachment because of being separated from his mother at a young age. Brad abhors out-of-control situations.

	Donna	Brad
C O P I N G	quiet channel surfing fluff pillows, bang on garage fridge not stick up for myself avoid mental hurt little depressed communication	Reassume myself Avoid - walk away from it Blaming shaming Projected voice Stone cold. faced "get the deck of cards together. put a rubber band on them"

COPING:

Donna handles her feelings by being quiet, watching a lot of TV, hitting pillows, and banging on the garage fridge. She gives in too easily and takes all the blame as she did for her parents' divorce. She becomes depressed and avoids her feelings. She eats unhealthy foods and gains weight, which adds to her blame when Brad does not want her sexually. She tries to communicate with Brad but eventually gives up.

Brad copes by blaming and shaming Donna. He keeps his feelings to himself and acts stone cold faced like he did when his father abused him. He keeps all his feelings tied up like a deck of cards tightly wrapped in a rubber band. His lack of emotion makes Donna experience abandonment. Brad experiences Donna's health as out-of-control and distances himself from her. At the same time, he demands to know where she is at any time of the day by paging her. He copes with scared feelings of abandonment (Donna's possible death) by contacting her incessantly.

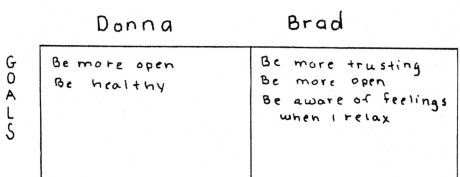

	Donna	Brad
G O A L S	Be more open Be healthy	Be more trusting Be more open Be aware of feelings when I relax

GOALS:

Donna decides to be more open and hopeful with Brad. She tells him when he is being over controlling and how she feels about his behavior. She stops taking all the blame. She starts working out with Brad at a local gym and eating healthy meals.

Brad understands and owns his over controlling behavior that stems from his early emotional injuries. He stops paging Donna ten times a day. He talks to her about his problems and worries at work. He becomes more relaxed about having to be constantly alert for any situation that might get out of control.

		Janet	Chris
E V E N T S		Chris not wanting me early marrage & affair at 20	Natural father verbally abusive Alcoholism I protected my mother from Dad
I S S U E S ← **F E E L I N G S**		Not wanted / rejected hurt, angry Can't fix it Sad, depressed, guilt Im not enough hurt, scared	Conflict scared sad Sameful Situation Sad, hurt, scared Can't fix it sad, scared, angry Waste time scared its not enough hurt, anger
	C O P I N G	cry talk yell throw something hit quiet sit in the patio + smoke make him happy	get out of situation until it blows over make plans to get away ask avoid quiet not talking "I want to just forget about it" improve it grumpy
	G O A L S	I'll get up w/ Chris I will get involved in a hobby or activity I will become more aware when my husband is scared + take it less personaly	Stop and conect w/ my wife I will make plans to go out with my wife alone every Friday I"ll make plans to stay out 1/mo. overnight w/ wife

4. CHRIS & JANET

Chris seeks treatment for himself. He recently separated from his wife of fifteen years and feels confused about their marriage. He is currently involved in another relationship. Chris works through his confusion and decides he wants his wife and family back. We see him alone five more times, and then with his wife eleven times. He returns home and they move with their two daughters to Oregon.

	Janet	Chris
E V E N T S	Chris not wanting me early marrage & affair at 20	Natural father verbally abusive <u>Alcoholism</u> I protected my mother from Dad

168

EVENTS:

Janet married Chris at age nineteen. They were passionate before their marriage. After their marriage, Chris showed a disinterest in sex. Janet experiences neglect like she did when her father worked too much. She feels hurt and angry and acts out her feelings by having a one-night stand with a friend of the family.

Chris is sexually functional when they do have sex. He states he just isn't as interested as he was before they got married. He starts to worry about the day-to-day concerns of his family. Just as he had played the sentry in his alcoholic family of origin, he acts overly vigilant when his wife becomes pregnant soon after their wedding day.

		Janet	Chris
I S S U E S	**F E E L I N G S**	Not wanted / rejected hurt, angry Can't fix it Sad, depressed, guilt Im not enough hurt, scared	conflict scared sad Sameful Situation Sad, hurt, scared Can't fix it Sad, scared, angry waste time scared its not enough hurt, anger

ISSUES/FEELINGS:

Janet develops Issues of not being wanted and of not being good enough. She tries over and over to get Chris to make love to her, with little result. He had shown interest and passion before she became pregnant, but now he only seems interested in work and ways to assure financial safety for the family.

Chris hates conflict and feels helpless when he can't fix problems in his family. He experiences a vague sense of anxiety when he isn't always busy doing something. This anxiety is the same anxiety he felt as a child in an alcoholic family.

	Janet	Chris
C O P I N G	cry talk yell throw something hit quiet sit in the patio + smoke make him happy	get out of situation until it blows over make plans to get away ask avoid quiet not talking "I want to just forget about it" improve it grumpy

COPING:

Janet handles her Feelings by trying to get Chris to talk about why he wasn't interested in her sexually. She yells, cries, throws things at him, and finally stays quiet and smokes cigarettes outside.

Chris stuffs his Feelings and tries to stay out of his wife's way. He just wants to forget about the conflict and wait until Janet cools off. His avoidance mirrors his early behavior in his alcoholic family of origin.

Janet	Chris
G O A L S	I'll get up w/ Chris I will get involved in a hobby or activity I will become more aware when my husband is scared + take it less personaly	Stop and conect w/ my wife I will make plans to go out with my wife alone every Friday I''ll make plans to stay out 1/mo. overnight w/ wife

GOALS:

Janet's Goals include getting up with Chris in the morning. He goes to bed early and gets up early because of his job. Chris uses his exhaustion at night to avoid his wife. By Janet getting up early and cuddling with Chris, it gives them time for a little love- making. She stops chasing him for communication. Janet gets involved in a church fund raiser and feels better about herself. She learns that her husband's fearful preoccupation with keeping the family financially safe arises from emotional injuries he experienced as a child, and not from him finding her unimportant.

Chris's main Goal is to connect with his wife in emotional and physical ways. He has to lessen his projects, stop acting like a sentry, and pay attention to his wife. He becomes responsible for planning a couple's night out every Friday and an overnight getaway once a month. As Chris stops playing the sentry, their relationship improves and their lovemaking increases.

CHAPTER EIGHT:
THE CHART AND TREATMENT

Let's very briefly look at how we use the Chart in therapeutic work.

We do initial interviews and written histories with the client or couple.

We include the use of a genogram at this point. It looks like a family tree.

We prepare a statement of the problem, diagnosis, treatment plan, and intervention for ourselves.

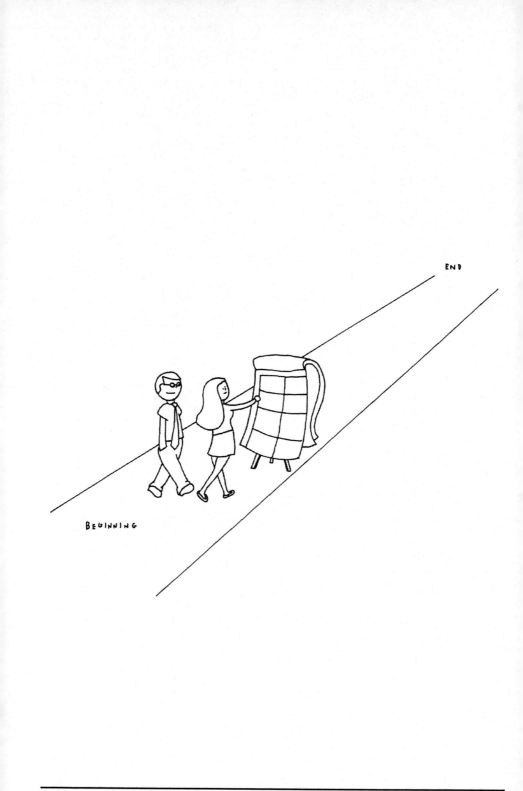

Once we establish a therapeutic relationship between ourselves and our clients, we use the Chart in the middle work of treatment.

Thereafter, we use the Chart every session by thumb tacking it up on the corkboard in our treatment office.

We refer to it when clients present new material relating to previous Charting.

We continuously update the Chart and develop new Events, Issues/Feelings, Coping, and Goals as they arise.

Sometimes we identify recent situations and behaviors as an extension of an Issue or Coping the client already identified on the Chart.

Remember the highway of the unconscious. We feel like we have traveled here before.

We help provide Tools to achieve Goals, once they are personally chosen and developed over the course of treatment.

We sometimes refer clients to groups and workshops while we are treating them.

We refer clients out for treatment when the tools they need are out of our scope of practice. For example: we would refer to a psychiatrist, who can prescribe medication, an individual we diagnose as having manic depression.

In the next chapter we explore an example session in which we develop a Chart for a married couple.

		Rebecca	Tom
I S S U E S	**E V E N T S**	2 miscarriages (12 wk hero child - good kid Stress disability (mom) Parents separated (age 12) for 3 mo.	2 miscarriages (12wks mom unavailable - Lost child Dad pedophile - step grandaughter (10
	F E E L I N G S	Perfection "good girl" Abandoned Scared, Sad Inadequate - never enough Anger	Neglect, abandoned "not cared about" sad, hurt, angry, scared Sexual issues
	C O P I N G	People pleaser eating defensive around feelings work hard, fast, + more	Withdrawing go to bed early TV sometimes, scowling look take it out on kids Arcades X movies
	G O A L S	weight watchers (12 wks Less defensive I wont let guilt drive my behavior Baby sitter every 2 wks	more open - vocal healthy eating Every 2 wks a date

CHAPTER NINE:
AN EXAMPLE CHART BUILDING SESSION

We provide an example how we do an initial Chart with a married couple. It takes place in their seventh session with us. We explored the usage of the Chart in a previous session.

The following case provides an example of the issue "I am unimportant."

The man comes from an alcoholic family where he was the "lost child."

Cyndy is Cyndy Thomas MSW, BCD.
Glenn is Glenn Thomas LCSW, BCD.
Rebecca is the wife.
Tom is the husband.

Cyndy: Hi. How's your week been?

Rebecca: It's been OK. We haven't been fighting much.

Glenn: Things have been a little easier.

Tom: We're doing better.

Glenn: If it's OK, we'd like to continue making your Chart. Is there anything that can't wait until later?

Rebecca: No, it's OK. We can start our chart.

Cyndy: Ok Tom?

Tom: Yeah.

Cyndy: Do you feel you both understand the sections?

Rebecca: Yeah, you explained the different sections last time.

Glenn: Tom, do you understand the way the chart is laid out?

Tom: Yeah Under Events, you can put she doesn't care about me.

Rebecca: I do care

about him. I'm just busy with this. I'm busy with that.

Glenn to Tom: We do know from your genogram you grew up a very quiet child who was neglected. Is that OK to put in your Event's section?

Tom: Yeah, I was definitely ignored.

Cyndy: I think your Issues here are neglect or unimportant. OK if we put that down in your Issues?

Tom: That seems right.

Glenn: What Feelings do you get when you feel unimportant?

Tom: I don't know, maybe hurt.

Cyndy (to Tom): That sensitivity comes from where you have been hurt before.

Tom: It's probably anger. At least I see the anger. I think the anger is down in there.

Glenn: How do you cope with those feelings? How would we know you were feeling those feelings?

Cyndy: What would you be doing? What behavior?

Tom: I withdraw.

Glenn: What do you withdraw into?

Tom: Just into myself, pretty much.

Rebecca: He just gets this scowl on his face. And you can see it in his face. But he tells me he is just fine.

Cyndy: But you know he is not fine.

Glenn: Does he withdraw into anything else? Like a book or TV?

Rebecca: Well, he used to withdraw into his alcohol and his drugs. Sometimes his TV. But usually, no, he just withdraws away from the family. He just goes into himself. Or he goes to bed early. He gets really tired.

Glenn: So we could put withdraw, scowl, avoid, past drug and alcohol usage into the Coping section of your chart?

Tom: Yes.

Cyndy: When you are pressing your feelings down, that does make you tired. It takes a lot of energy to keep those feelings down. You feel depressed. And you might feel like just going to bed. (To Rebecca) And you can tell something is the matter. But it's hard to know what it really could be. Could it be work? Could it be the kids? Could it be me?

Rebecca: He seems so far away. It feels like something I should fix.

Cyndy: If you knew what it would be.

Glenn: You are sounding very co-dependent.

Rebecca: I understand that.

Glenn: I'm glad you notice that.

Cyndy: You say sometimes he is scowling?

Glenn: Anything else

you might be doing if you are experiencing being neglected? Any other ways you withdraw?

Tom: I get angry at the kids more.

Cyndy: Do you take it out on the kids?

Rebecca: I think we both do to a degree. We both have less tolerance.

Cyndy: So sometimes you give some expression of your anger to the kids. The stuff that normally wouldn't bother you does. Can we put "Give anger to the kids" into the Coping section of your Chart?

Tom: Yeah.

Cyndy: Keep in mind this is similar to the family you grew up in. Your dad was explosive when he drank. But I don't think the intensity is the same. But it is a little bit like it. The same behaviors. We learn our behaviors from the families we grew up in.

Glenn: Do you remember what you did as a

kid? Did you do the same things when you felt neglected or left out that you do now?

Tom: Yeah, I did.

Glenn: You don't have many memories of your childhood, do you?

Tom: No.

Rebecca: When I met him, he was extremely withdrawn. He was very moody. There were times we would have a lot of fun. And then he would get into these moods. I couldn't get him to talk. It would take him 30 minutes to say one sentence. He would just sit there and pout.

Cyndy: What would you see that would trigger it?

Tom: When I'm being ignored.

Cyndy: You might feel slightly neglected, and that could trigger it. You back up and withdraw into yourself.

Rebecca: I thought it had to do with me. I

thought it had to do with him feeling I was not the right person for him.

Cyndy: Sounds like a strong Issue for you, Rebecca. Can we put "Not good enough" as an Issue for you in your chart?

Rebecca: OK, that seems right.

Glenn: What do you feel when you aren't good enough? Look up at the list of the Six Basic Feelings. Which ones would you pick?

Rebecca: Mostly hurt and scared.

Glenn: Can I put those under your Issue of "Not Good Enough"?

Rebecca: OK.

Tom: That was then, not now.

Rebecca: Do you feel I am the right person for you now?

Tom: Yeah, I do feel like you are the right person for me. I also feel like I am alone sometimes.

Glenn: You present

some strong sexual acting out. Do you ever feel alone sexually? I bring it up because in the past you would go to sex arcades when you felt alone.

Tom: Yeah, I go there for release.

Glenn: Did you have sex with anyone when you were there?

Tom: No, I won't do that anymore. It's not safe.

Glenn: At another time we can take a detailed sexual history of you (Tom). For now lets continue with the sex arcades.

Rebecca: The night that you went there, when we had the fight on the phone. That was like instant. You were angry at me. And you stayed there for three hours.

Glenn: Let's take a look at that. Because what Rebecca is saying is that you get mad and then you go to sex arcades.

Tom: Yeah, but she told me not to go home.

Glenn: But why did you choose that instead of somewhere else to go? Maybe it's as simple as you say. Maybe it's something else.

Rebecca: You could have just called me and asked me if I had calmed down.

Tom: I had just never been there. I wanted to check it out. It was by our house.

Cyndy: I think it's connected to your Coping. It's connected to your release just as you said.

It's so much of a coincidence. You felt angry and hurt and went to a sex arcade where you could feel excited instead. Can I put sex arcade as Coping for you?

Tom: Yes.

Glenn: Another way to understand it is why did you do it just after a fight with your wife?

Tom: I was just driving home. It was just off to the side of the road.

Glenn (to Rebecca): You don't think so.

Rebecca: I think it's, "Oh yeah. I will just show her!" I mean how many times have you not been mad at me and you never stopped there before. And you picked that time. That day that we had a fight. I think you were trying to punish me.

Glenn: Maybe you just thought you had more license to do it. You were mad. But it also has an addictive flavor to it. You did it in a time of stress. You feel rejected, sad, and angry. You put a sex arcade into your brain. You drown yourself in sexual excitement.

Rebecca: Yeah, maybe you just gave yourself permission. You had an excuse. I don't know. But I don't think it's a simple matter of, "Oh look, maybe I'll just go in there." I don't think it was exactly like that. I am glad you told me about it.

Tom: I just drove by. I did feel better after I stopped.

Glenn: Well, it's something to put on the back burner. Just think about.

Cyndy: Yeah, I agree. It might be something you aren't aware of as you are doing it. You might not be really conscious about it. "But it seems like she doesn't care about me anyway. She doesn't even want me to come home. So heck, I'll just go here." And you're not aware of how hurt she would be. Especially since she told you not to go home. It really hits your Issue. You don't have to listen to her. You could just go home anyway. You don't have to do what she says. You could tell her, "You can't tell me to not come home. I want to get this settled." Because you know she is mad when she says that. She doesn't really mean it. It's a way she can hurt you. It's coming out of her anger. Because on some level both of you know each other very well. You know where the injuries are. You may not be aware of it. But it would be one of the most hurtful things you could be told. "I don't want you."

Glenn: Let me ask you, Tom, do you think that by going to the sex arcade, your wife would be mad or hurt by it?

Tom: Yeah.

Glenn: Then there has to be something connected there. Maybe at that point you were angry and you didn't care what she felt. Or it could be a pay back, a way to cope with your anger. You were angry and what you did with that anger was take it into the sex arcade. You paid your wife back and washed your anger away with sex.

Cyndy: Yeah, like "You hurt me, so I'm going to hurt you." The more you are aware of what your behavior means, the more you can understand each other. Neither one of you is a bad person. We all say stuff that's hurtful when we're angry. Everybody does that. It's really a way to back the other person off. When you are hurt, you want to hurt back. I'm glad that was brought up. To me it all seems connected. I think when we piece together both of your Issues, it will all make sense.

Glenn: It's common for people to do things that make the other person mad indirectly. And because you are withdrawn, you are not as active. You might do things that would make her angry, but not directly. You may be indirect. You are angry. She is not available. You want to spend time with her. She is working a lot or spending her free time with the kids. You feel neglected. You feel angry about it. You are not as direct about it. You let it bottle up inside you and then at times you become abusive. Especially when you drink.

Cyndy: "Bottle it up!" Listen to how that phrase has a double meaning for you, Tom.

Glenn: You could do it differently. When you are feeling neglected, you could say to her, "I feel like you are spending too much time at work and with the kids. It hurts me when you don't spend any quality time with me. I want you to stay up tonight and talk with me." That's direct. Passive aggressive is doing things that make another person mad or hurt when you are mad. You may not be completely aware of it. You come home real late. You know it will make her mad. But you don't tell her directly what you are feeling. You may have a tendency to be passive aggressive.

Tom: Yeah, I think I do.

Glenn: Let's put "being indirect with my feelings" in your Coping section. OK?

Tom: It's OK.

Cyndy: It's a way to get the aggression out. But it's a more passive way to do it. And I think your style tends to be more like that. You still have Feelings and Rebecca needs to hear what they are. And sometimes you are angry and it really doesn't have anything to do with Rebecca. But it's hard for her to figure that out without you saying, "It's not you I'm mad at. A guy backed into my car. Whatever. A hundred and one things can happen in life. It's not anything to do with you. I'm just so mad." And then Rebecca would want to fix it. She would agree, "Yeah I would be mad too." Then you get it out. But if you stuff your anger in and withdraw, eventually it will come out somewhere. It's going to leak out. Maybe when you slam the refrigerator really hard. When your son does something wrong. It's just a vehicle for expression. A fight. Just to get the expression out. When you think about it afterwards, you realize it was so dumb. A fight over lettuce or tomatoes.

Rebecca: That's almost as stupid as our fight was.

Cyndy: It was a way to get some expression.

Rebecca: I was just picking a fight with him on

the phone. And I was. I was mad and I didn't even know what I was mad about.

Cyndy: You were needing expression. Did you figure out what it was? Was it lots of things?

Rebecca: I don't even know.

Cyndy: Is your style to hold in and take care of everybody else?

Rebecca: Yeah.

Glenn: When we look at your side, we see you grew up in an alcoholic family.

Rebecca: Yeah. (Looks at Tom) Do you think so? (Tom nods) Yeah, I think so. I don't know if my father is still drinking. He has diabetes now so I don't know if he is still drinking. I haven't been up there for a year.

Glenn: Do you know the different child types in an alcoholic family?

Cyndy: Like the "Perfect Child"?

Rebecca: I'm probably the Hero. I was the one who got the better grades. I was the good kid. My brother was the one who caused a lot of grief for my parents.

Cyndy: You were the good one.

Rebecca: Yeah, I was the good one.

Glenn: So the Issue would be "Perfection," the Event would be the "Hero child in an alcoholic family," and the Coping would be "holding it in." Is it OK to put all that on your Chart?

Rebecca: Yes, go ahead.

Cyndy: You saved the day. You were the rescuer.

Glenn: So when you are not being good, what Feelings do you get?

Rebecca: Probably ashamed that I'm not adequate enough.

Cyndy: That's like guilt. What about under the guilt? Under that shame, what Feeling would you have?

Rebecca: There's a lot of sadness. There's probably a lot of scared feelings. I think what I'm really afraid of is that people won't like me anymore.

Cyndy: So can we put sadness, scared, and guilty under your Issue of Perfection?

Rebecca: Yeah, that fits.

Glenn: I think Abandonment is another Issue for you.

Cyndy: So if you aren't perfect, you will be abandoned.

Rebecca: That's right. (Starts crying)
Cyndy: Just talking about it really touches you.

Rebecca: I don't know what's the matter with me.

Cyndy: You just got touched by the Issue. You both have similar Issues, but different lives. So as long as you are perfect, nobody could find any reason to leave you. You want to be the best mom, the best client, the best little girl.

Rebecca: I'm a people pleaser.

Glenn: Under your Coping section, let's put "please people." And let's put Abandonment as another Issue on the chart. That's really a core issue for you.

Cyndy: That Feeling is absolutely terrifying for you.

Rebecca: I don't know why it's that way. I was just a little kid.

Cyndy: You were scared to make any mistakes. If you were just perfect, your dad wouldn't drink so much. But your family is going to be different because you are going to change it. And little kids have to make mistakes so they can learn. And yet you tried too hard to be so perfect and good.

Rebecca: Everyone, even my grandparents, say I am the loving one of the whole family. My mother got disability for stress.

Glenn: Your mother got disability for stress?

Rebecca: She got it from her job. She worked as a communications specialist with the county.

Glenn: How did she show her stress?

Rebecca: She didn't show her stress at home. She didn't show things to us. My parents separated and the first we knew my parents had fights was when my mother told us Dad had moved out. I had to go to his closet and check to see if his clothes were there because I didn't believe it.

Glenn: How old were you?

Rebecca: When my mom and dad separated? They were only separated for three or four months. I was twelve, in junior high. We never even heard them fight. We never thought they had any problems at all. The way I was brought up, my parents came home and had cocktails before dinner all the time. Mom doesn't drink hardly anymore. So I don't think she would be classified as an alcoholic.

Cyndy: Usually a person is alcoholic for life and either a dry or a wet alcoholic.

Glenn: We know you had an alcoholic dad at home. And mother was coming home all stressed out. And they were both using alcohol. They both drank.

Rebecca: Oh yeah, they drank. In the evenings. But they weren't alcoholics. My mom was... my mom was (long pause) never really there for me when I was an adolescent, when I started questioning life and things like that. It was my dad who would have debates and arguments with me. And my grandmother would talk about issues and government and politics and religion, and my father would too. My mother would not discuss anything like that. I feel really connected to my mom now. But back then, I thought she was very controlling and manipulative. And a very prudish person. I remember thinking all through high school that she wanted to control everything.

Cyndy: She tried to be right?

Glenn: She sounds scared.

Rebecca: Yeah. She had a need to know this is what you will do and what you won't do. And that's that. She would never discuss sex with us. I thought she was prudish. She was not very functional. But she has grown a lot.

Cyndy: She has changed. You know in your own marriage how much it takes to get a separation. It just takes a lot to separate. You have to go through a lot. Have you ever separated?

Rebecca: No.

Cyndy: And to go into the closet to see if dad's clothes are still there. You didn't have a clue what was happening. That's a shock. That's like, "Where's dad? Where are his clothes?

And I feel pretty close to him. Wasn't I good enough for him to stay?"

Rebecca: He moved out when I was in junior high, before I really got close to him. It was in high school where I felt really close to him

Glenn: Let's bring it back to the present. How would we know you were experiencing feeling inadequate? What kind of things would you be doing? When you start to feel like you might be seen as inad-

equate, what would you be doing?

Rebecca: Besides eating? (Nervous laugh) I get defensive, I guess. Angry. I get really defensive and angry. I've got to defend myself.

Cyndy: Can we put "eating, get defensive, and angry" in your Coping section?

Rebecca: Yeah, that's right.

Glenn: We know you spend a lot of time at work. Do you ever work harder, faster, more?

Rebecca: Oh yeah, at work.

Tom: Definitely.

Rebecca: Yeah I'll just work harder and faster.

Glenn: Can we put that in your Coping section?

Rebecca: Yeah.

Tom: I wish you would do that at home.

Rebecca: Yeah you do. See how I feel inadequate?

Cyndy: You feel like it's not enough? Like whatever you do is not good enough?

Glenn: You might look around the house. Maybe you don't keep it up because you are mad at Tom.

Rebecca: Yeah, sometimes I don't care.

Glenn: Being a good girl. Is a good girl sexual too? There is such a strong dynamic in that Tom is so out-of-control sexually. I wonder if there is a complementary on your side? A good girl who doesn't want sex?

Rebecca: I don't know. I don't know. That's a good question.

Tom: I don't think she has any interest in sex whatsoever.

Rebecca: You keep telling me that. But I used to be very interested. So I don't appreciate him telling me that.

Cyndy: Do you sometimes think that good girls or nice girls aren't supposed to like sex or initiate sex or really take a lot of interest in being sexual?

Glenn: Right. Is it that you want to please someone else instead of wanting your own pleasure? Do you take care of the other person instead of owning your own sexuality? It's a big issue in the couple because Tom's out-of-control and Rebecca's in control.

Rebecca: It's not like he is my first sexual partner. I wasn't promiscuous. But I had a few relationships before Tom.

Cyndy: How are you with initiating? Like when you feel sexy? Or when you want to feel close?

Rebecca: It's been so long since I've felt a need to be close. But I do initiate times to be together.

Cyndy: Who initiates it the most?

Rebecca: I think he will say he does. But I think he doesn't at all. Since his use of alcohol and drugs, we've been trying to get well from that. (Starts crying) You can't ignore a person all week long and suddenly that night say, "Well tonight we have a half an hour with the kids down."

Glenn: Thats very true. Also, the big issue is trust. The past has been a lot of pain.

Cyndy: Because that could make like an imprint, it could make it hard for you to initiate and want and be a people pleaser.

Glenn: You have so many overlays. It would be really clean if you felt a lot of safety and trust. You were feeling much closer and feeling true intimacy. If that was happening and you still felt you weren't initiating and weren't feeling sexual, we'd be looking for the "good girl." But with so many overlays, it's more complex.

Cyndy: It seems it could be a little bit of all those things. And as you feel closer in the relationship, you will probably feel sexier. But I would agree with Glenn that it stands out so much that there must be another part to it.

Glenn: You see Tom's behavior has been so out of control and you have been trying to stay in so much control like in your family of origin. You don't want to wake up and find his closet empty.

Cyndy: And for you to feel safe enough and trusting enough, you could lose control and be vulnerable. In view of what's been happening, it's very difficult for you to be that open.

Glenn: Then you have a cycle where Tom is feeling more and more neglected and the way that Tom Copes is to turn to drinking. That affects Rebecca's safety and trust Issues and she withdraws into her work and the kids, which then touches your Feelings of neglect, and so on.
Rebecca: We have had a few attempts at intimacy in the past months. And the last time was at my suggestion. We gave the kids to a baby sitter and checked into a motel. A change of pace from the house. On one level it was the closest I have felt to him in a long time. But he hasn't been able to have an orgasm. (Crying) It just touched my feelings of inadequacy. And it's harder for me to go back and try again and again. How many times can we try? I understand it just wasn't bad. In fact it was a great evening. Again we mostly connected, but we haven't in a long time. I feel like I was stabbed. Two days later he wants to initiate

things again and I just don't feel like doing it. I was just raw emotionally. And hurt.

Cyndy: Like something was wrong with you because Tom didn't orgasm.

Rebecca: Yeah.

Glenn: If we look up at your Chart, we see "Not good enough" and "Hurt." What did you do to Cope with your Feelings?

Rebecca: I got defensive and angry.

Glenn: Was that typical for you, Tom? Are you slow to orgasm?

Tom: No, just recently.

Glenn: You have to work with what's normal for you.

Cyndy: Can you maintain an erection? Or are you able to start and then lose an erection?

Tom: Yeah, sometimes.

Cyndy: Or sometimes does it just take you longer? What can be normal for one person isn't necessarily normal for another.

Rebecca: He doesn't have any problem once he gets started.

Glenn: And for you Rebecca, what does it feel like when he is unable to orgasm or get an erection?

Rebecca: I feel like a failure.

Glenn: A hero is supposed to be able to do anything.

Cyndy: Do you feel hurt?

Rebecca: Yeah.

Cyndy: We can see that Feeling under your Issue "Not good enough." Hurt doesn't go with excited or happy. So you feel hurt and you won't feel happy and excited.

Glenn: Oops, look at the time. I'm sorry, we are going to have to stop now. But we will get out the Chart next time and keep working on it. We've already starting using it when we referred back several times to an Issue or Coping you identified.

Cyndy: As we work on your chart, you will get a clearer picture of where you came from. When we get to your Goals, you'll have a clearer idea of where you want to go.

CLOSING

We have reached the end of the book. We thank you for reading it.

Each person sets his or her own course for self-discovery. Some have this value of self-discovery, others do not. It was for the former we wrote this book. A courageous person is the one who looks within and through the exploration suffers and eventually rises.

ABOUT THE AUTHOR

Glenn Thomas is a licensed clinical social worker and board certified diplomate, who has practiced for over 25 years. He graduated with a bachelors in General Science from the University of Washington, and received a Masters degree in Social Work from California State University at Fresno. He has practiced as a child therapist and worked specializing as a family therapist, working with couples for many years. He has written three software titles published by two education software publishers. Glenn created the **loveandencourage.com** web site to inform, teach, and help. Glenn works as a social worker and practices with his wife, Cyndy, who is also a licensed clinical social worker and board certified diplomate, in a private practice based in Saratoga, CA. He has four adult stepchildren he adores.